Friend *noun*

Definition of *friend*

: one attached to another by affection or esteem
　　　// She's my best *friend*.

: a favoured companion

Let's be honest, there's only one reason you bought this book and that's as a gift to your best friend, probably because you've upset them in some way and want to get back into their good books. So, let's get it out the way. Here's the part where you can dedicate it to them.

THIS BOOK IS FOR

_____

**THANK YOU FOR BEING THE BEST FRIEND
EVER.
LOVE FROM,**

_____

"A good friend can tell you what the matter with you is in a minute. He may not seem such a good friend after telling."
– Arthur Brisbane

"I would rather walk with a friend in the dark, than alone in the light."
– Helen Keller

"A true friend is someone who thinks that you are a good egg even though he knows that you are slightly cracked."
– Bernard Meltzer

"A true friend stabs you in the front."
– Oscar Wilde

"There is nothing better than a friend, unless it is a friend with chocolate. "
– Linda Grayson

"The most beautiful discovery true friends make is that they can grow separately without growing apart."
– Elisabeth Foley

"Find a group of people who challenge and inspire you; spend a lot of time with them, and it will change your life."
– Amy Poehler

"Lots of people want to ride with you in the limo, but what you want is someone who will take the bus with you when the limo breaks down."
– Oprah Winfrey

"When you stop expecting people to be perfect, you can like them for who they are."
– Donald Miller

"Do not keep on with a mockery of friendship after the substance is gone — but part, while you can part friends. Bury the carcass of friendship: it is not worth embalming."
– William Hazlitt

"Each friend represents a world in us, a world possibly not born until they arrive, and it is only by this meeting that a new world is born."
– Anais Nin

Anything is possible when you have the right people there to support you.
– Misty Copeland

"If you make friends with yourself you will never be alone."
– Maxwell Maltz

"We come from homes far from perfect, so you end up almost parent and sibling to your friends – your own chosen family. There's nothing like a really loyal, dependable, good friend. Nothing."
– Jennifer Aniston

"Sometimes being a friend means mastering the art of timing. There is a time for silence. A time to let go and allow people to hurl themselves into their own destiny. And a time to prepare to pick up the pieces when it's all over."
– Octavia Butler

"Friendship is the source of the greatest pleasures, and without friends even the most agreeable pursuits become tedious."
– Thomas Aquinas

"Friendship is a plant of slow growth and must undergo and withstand the shocks of adversity before it is entitled to the appellation."
– George Washington

A friend is one who overlooks your broken fence and admires the flowers in your garden.
– Unknown

"A friend is one that knows you as you are, understands where you have been, accepts what you have become, and still, gently allows you to grow."
– William Shakespeare

"A sweet friendship refreshes the soul."
– Proverbs 27:9

"Some people arrive and make such a beautiful impact on your life, you can barely remember what life was like without them."
– **Anna Taylor**

"The greatest compliment that was ever paid me was when someone asked me what I thought, and attended to my answer."
– **Henry David Thoreau**

"Many a person has held close, throughout their entire lives, two friends that always remained strange to one another, because one of them attracted by virtue of similarity, the other by difference."
– **Emil Ludwig**

"People are lonely because they build walls instead of bridges."
– Joseph F. Newton Men

"Friendship is like a glass ornament, once it is broken it can rarely be put back together exactly the same way."
– Charles Kingsley

"An insincere and evil friend is more to be feared than a wild beast; a wild beast may wound your body, but an evil friend will wound your mind."
– Buddha

"A friend knows the song in my heart and sings it to me when my memory fails."
– Donna Roberts

Try to be a rainbow in someone's cloud.
– Maya Angelou

"A friend is someone who makes it easy to believe in yourself."
– Heidi Wills

"I no doubt deserved my enemies, but I don't believe I deserved my friends."
– Walt Whitman

"In prosperity our friends know us; in adversity, we know our friends."
– John Churton Collins

"It is the friends you can call up at 4 a.m. that matter."
– Marlene Dietrich

"Things are never quite as scary when you have a best friend."
– Bill Watterson

"Sometimes being a friend means mastering the art of timing. There is a time for silence. A time to let go and allow people to hurl themselves into their own destiny. And a time to prepare to pick up the pieces when it's all over."
– Gloria Naylor

"Fate chooses your relations, you choose your friends."
– Jacques Delille

"There is magic in long-distance friendships. They let you relate to other human beings in a way that goes beyond being physically together and is often more profound."
– Diana Cortes

"Friends should be like books, few, but hand-selected."
– C.J. Langenhoven

"Someone to tell it to is one of the fundamental needs of human beings."
– Miles Franklin

"Do not save your loving speeches for your friends till they are dead; do not write them on their tombstones, speak them rather now instead."
– Anna Cummins

"It is not so much our friends' help that helps us, as the confidence of their help."
– Epicurus

"A friend is someone who knows all about you and still loves you."
– Elbert Hubbard

"The tender friendships one gives up, on parting, leave their bite on the heart, but also a curious feeling of a treasure somewhere buried."
– Antoine de Saint-Exupéry

"A friend is one of the nicest things you can have, and one of the best things you can be."
– Douglas Pagels

"Do I not destroy my enemies when I make them my friends?"
– Abraham Lincoln

It's not that diamonds are a girl's best friend, but it's your best friends who are your diamonds.
– Gina Barreca

"A friend is a person with whom I may be sincere. Before him I may think aloud. I am arrived at last in the presence of a man so real and equal, that I may drop even those undermost garments of dissimulation, courtesy, and second thought, which men never put off, and may deal with him with the simplicity and wholeness with which one chemical atom meets another."
– Ralph Waldo Emerson

"Life is partly what we make it, and partly what it is made by the friends we choose."
– Tennessee Williams

"A snowball in the face is surely the perfect beginning to a lasting friendship."
– Markus Zusak

"If it's very painful for you to criticise your friends — you're safe in doing it. But if you take the slightest pleasure in it, that's the time to hold your tongue."
– **Alice Duer Miller**

"Blessed are they who have the gift of making friends, for it is one of God's greatest gifts. It involves many things, but above all the power of going out of one's self and appreciating what is noble and loving in another."
– **Thomas Hughes**

"Every friendship goes through ups and downs. Dysfunctional patterns set in; external situations cause internal friction; you grow apart and then bounce back together."
– **Mariella Frostrup**

"The best time to make friends is before you need them."
– Ethel Barrymore

"In the sweetness of friendship let there be laughter, for in the dew of little things the heart finds its morning and is refreshed."
– Khalil Gibran

"If you have one true friend you have more than your share."
– Thomas Fuller

In the cookie of life, friends are the chocolate chips.
– Unknown

"Be slow in choosing a friend, slower in changing."
– Benjamin Franklin

"One of the tasks of true friendship is to listen compassionately and creatively to the hidden silences. Often secrets are not revealed in words, they lie concealed in the silence between the words or in the depth of what is unsayable between two people."
– John O'Donohue

"Nothing makes the earth seem so spacious as to have friends at a distance; they make the latitudes and longitudes."
– Henry David Thoreau

"Men kick friendship around like a football, but it doesn't seem to crack. Women treat it like glass and it goes to pieces."
– Anne Morrow Lindbergh

"They may forget what you said, but they will never forget how you made them feel."
– Carl W. Buechner

"Truly great friends are hard to find, difficult to leave, and impossible to forget."
– Unknown

"A true friend is one who overlooks your failures and tolerates your success!"
– Doug Larson

"Of all the things which wisdom provides to make us entirely happy, much the greatest is the possession of friendship."
– Epicurus

"Where there are friends, there is wealth."
– Titus Maccius Plautus

"A true friend is someone who is there for you when he'd rather be anywhere else."
– Len Wein

"There is a friend in the life of each of us who seems not a separate person, however dear and beloved, but an expansion, an interpretation, of one's self, the very meaning of soul."
– Edith Wharton

"True friends are like diamonds – bright, beautiful, valuable, and always in style."
– Unknown

"Don't walk in front of me; I may not follow. Don't walk behind me; I may not lead. Just walk beside me and be my friend."
– Albert Camus

"The friend who can be silent with us in a moment of despair or confusion, who can stay with us in an hour of grief and bereavement, who can tolerate not knowing… not healing, not curing… that is a friend who cares."
– Henri Nouwen

"The royal road to a man's heart is to talk to him about the things he treasures most."
– Dale Carnegie

"To the world you may be just one person, but to one person you may be the world."
– Brandi Snyder

"Without friends no one would choose to live, though he had all other goods."
– Aristotle

"There is nothing on this earth more to be prized than true friendship."
– Thomas Aquinas

"A best friend is someone who makes you laugh even when you think you'll never smile again."
– Unknown

"Friends show their love in times of trouble, not in happiness."
– Euripides

"Friendship is always a sweet responsibility, never an opportunity."
– Khalil Gibran

"A real friend is one who walks in when the rest of the world walks out."
– Walter Winchell

"The great thing about new friends is that they bring new energy to your soul."
– Shanna Rodriguez

"If you live to be 100, I hope I live to be 100 minus 1 day, so I never have to live without you."
– Winnie the Pooh

"A good friend is a connection to life — a tie to the past, a road to the future, the key to sanity in a totally insane world."
– Lois Wyse

"Friendship marks a life even more deeply than love. Love risks degenerating into obsession, friendship is never anything but sharing."
– Elie Wiesel

"Everyone has a friend during each stage of life. But only lucky ones have the same friend in all stages of life."
– Unknown

"I like to listen. I have learned a great deal from listening carefully. Most people never listen."
– Ernest Hemingway

"I cannot even imagine where I would be today were it not for that handful of friends who have given me a heart full of joy. Let's face it, friends make life a lot more fun."
– Charles R. Swindoll

"Friendship improves happiness, and abates misery, by doubling our joys, and dividing our grief."
– Marcus Tullius Cicero

"Love is blind; friendship closes its eyes."
– Friedrich Nietzsche

"Friendship is born at that moment when one person says to another, 'What! You too? I thought I was the only one."
– C.S. Lewis

"It takes a long time to grow an old friend."
– John Leonard

"All love that has not friendship for its base, is like a mansion built upon the sand."
– Ella Wheeler Wilcox

"True friendship comes when the silence between two people is comfortable."
– David Tyson

"Friendship consists in forgetting what one gives and remembering what one receives."
– Alexander Dumas

"It is one of the blessings of old friends that you can afford to be stupid with them."
– Ralph Waldo Emerson

"There is a magnet in your heart that will attract true friends. That magnet is unselfishness, thinking of others first; when you learn to live for others, they will live for you."
– Paramahansa Yogananda

"Sitting silently beside a friend who is hurting may be the best gift we can give."
– Unknown

"Sweet is the memory of distant friends!
Like the mellow rays of the departing sun,
it falls tenderly, yet sadly, on the heart."
– Washington Irving

"Only a true best friend can protect you
from your immortal enemies."
– Richelle Mead

"Friends are the siblings God never gave
us."
– Mencius

"True friendship ought never to conceal
what it thinks."
– St. Jerome

"There's not a word yet for old friends
who've just met."
– Jim Henson

"One of the most beautiful qualities of true friendship is to understand and to be understood."
– Lucius Annaeus Seneca

"Every friendship travels at some time through the black valley of despair. This tests every aspect of your affection. You lose the attraction and the magic."
– John O'Donohue

"If you have two friends in your lifetime, you're lucky. If you have one good friend, you're more than lucky."
– S.E. Hinton

"A single rose can be my garden… a single friend, my world."
– Leo Buscaglia

"One friend with whom you have a lot in common is better than three with whom you struggle to find things to talk about."
– Mindy Kaling

"Friendship is when people know all about you but like you anyway."
– Unknown

"Friendship multiplies the good of life and divides the evil."
– Baltasar Gracian

"Don't make friends who are comfortable to be with. Make friends who will force you to lever yourself up."
– Thomas J. Watson

"Friends: people who borrow my books and set wet glasses on them."
– Edwin Arlington Robinson

"You can make more friends in two months by becoming interested in other people than you can in two years by trying to get other people interested in you."
— **Dale Carnegie**

"A friend can tell you things you don't want to tell yourself."
— **Frances Ward Weller**

"A friend is someone who understands your past, believes in your future, and accepts you just the way you are."
– **Unknown**

"Friendship is a wildly underrated medication."
– **Anna Deavere Smith**

"How many slams in an old screen door? Depends how loud you shut it. How many slices in a bread? Depends how thin you cut it. How much good inside a day? Depends how good you live 'em. How much love inside a friend? Depends how much you give 'em."
– Shel Silverstein

"Ultimately the bond of all companionship, whether in marriage or in friendship, is conversation."
– Oscar Wilde

"Remember that the most valuable antiques are dear old friends."
– H. Jackson Brown Jr.

"True friends don't judge each other, they judge other people together."
– Emilie Saint-Genis

"A friend is someone who gives you total freedom to be yourself — and especially to feel, or not feel. Whatever you happen to be feeling at any moment is fine with them. That's what real love amounts to – letting a person be what he really is."
– **Jim Morrison**

"I think if I've learned anything about friendship, it's to hang in, stay connected, fight for them, and let them fight for you. Don't walk away, don't be distracted, don't be too busy or tired, don't take them for granted. Friends are part of the glue that holds life and faith together. Powerful stuff."
– **John Katz**

"Friendship is a pretty full-time occupation if you really are friendly with somebody. You can't have too many friends because then you're just not really friends."
– Truman Capote

"Real friendship is when your friend comes over to your house and then you both just take a nap."
– Unknown

"Some people go to priests, others to poetry, I to my friends."
– Virginia Woolf

"Since there is nothing so well worth having as friends, never lose a chance to make them."
– Francesco Guicciardini

"What you do not want done to yourself, do not do to others."
– Confucius

"A true friend never gets in your way unless you happen to be going down."
– Arnold H. Glasgow

"I don't need a friend who changes when I change and who nods when I nod; my shadow does that much better."
– Plutarch

"True friends are never apart, maybe in distance but never in heart."
– Unknown

"A friend to all is a friend to none."
– Aristotle

"In everyone's life, at some time, our inner fire goes out. It is then burst into flame by an encounter with another human being. We should all be thankful for those people who rekindle the inner spirit."
– Albert Schweitzer

"There is nothing I wouldn't do for those who are really my friends. I have no notion of loving people by halves; it is not my nature."
– Jane Austen

"I value the friend who for me finds time on his calendar, but I cherish the friend who for me does not consult his calendar."
– Robert Brault

"A friend is a gift you give yourself."
– Robert Louis Stevenson

"The real test of friendship is can you literally do nothing with the other person? Can you enjoy those moments of life that are utterly simple?"
– Eugene Kennedy

There are friends, there is family, and then there are friends that become family.
– Unknown

"A loyal friend laughs at your jokes when they're not so good, and sympathises with your problems when they're not so bad."
– Arnold H. Glasgow

"It is not a lack of love, but a lack of friendship that makes unhappy marriages."
– Friedrich Nietzsche

"The language of friendship is not words but meanings."
– Henry David Thoreau

"Friendship is the hardest thing in the world to explain. It's not something you learn in school. But if you haven't learned the meaning of friendship, you really haven't learned anything."
– Muhammad Ali

"Don't be dismayed at good-byes. A farewell is necessary before you can meet again. And meeting again, after moments or lifetimes, is certain for those who are friends."
– Richard Bach

"True friendship is never serene."
– Marquise de Sevigne

"Growing apart doesn't change the fact that for a long time we grew side by side; our roots will always be tangled. I'm glad for that."
– Ally Condie

"There are no rules for friendship. It must be left to itself. We cannot force it any more than love."
– William Hazlitt

"It's not what we have in life, but who we have in our life that matters."
– Unknown

"Friends confront each other sometimes, and sometimes the friendship lasts, and sometimes it doesn't."
– Brooke Elliott

"Many people will walk in and out of your life, but only true friends will leave footprints in your heart."
– Eleanor Roosevelt

"Wishing to be friends is quick work, but friendship is a slow ripening fruit."
– Aristotle

"One's friends are that part of the human race with which one can be human."
– George Santayana

"Be slow to fall into friendship; but when thou art in, continue firm and constant."'
– Socrates

"Friendship is a strong and habitual inclination in two persons to promote the good and happiness of one another."
– Eustace Budgell

"Sometimes being with your best friend is all the therapy you need."
— **Unknown**

"One measure of friendship consists not in the number of things friends can discuss, but in the number of things they need no longer mention."
— **Clifton Fadiman**

"Tis the privilege of friendship to talk nonsense, and to have her nonsense respected."
— **Charles Lamb**

"Friendship is the purest love."
— **Osho**

"Let us be grateful to the people who make us happy; they are the charming gardeners who make our souls blossom."
– Marcel Proust

"Some souls just understand each other upon meeting."
– N. R. Hart

"When the world is so complicated, the simple gift of friendship is within all of our hands."
– Maria Shriver

Good friends are like stars. You don't always see them, but you know they're always there.
– Unknown

"Life is an awful, ugly place to not have a best friend."
– Sarah Desse

True friends are always together in spirit.
– L. M. Montgomery

"If you go looking for a friend, you're going to find they're very scarce. If you go out to be a friend, you'll find them everywhere."
– Zig Ziglar

"In the End, we will remember not the words of our enemies, but the silence of our friends."
– Martin Luther King, Jr.

"You can always tell a real friend: when you've made a fool of yourself, he doesn't feel you've done a permanent job."
– Laurence J. Peter

"Keep away from those who try to belittle your ambitions. Small people always do that, but the really great make you believe that you too can become great."
– Mark Twain

"True friendship is like sound health; the value of it is seldom known until it is lost."
– Charles Caleb Colton

"Never leave a friend behind. Friends are all we have to get us through this life–and they are the only things from this world that we could hope to see in the next."
– Dean Koontz

"No person is your friend who demands your silence, or denies your right to grow."
– Alice Walker

"Flatter me, and I may not believe you. Criticise me, and I may not like you. Ignore me, and I may not forgive you. Encourage me, and I will not forget you. Love me and I may be forced to love you."
– William Arthur Ward

"A man's friendships are one of the best measures of his worth."
– Charles Darwin

"One loyal friend is worth ten thousand relatives."
– Euripides

"Life was meant for good friends and great adventures."
– Unknown

"A friendship that can end never really began."
– Publilius Syrus

"Awards become corroded. Friends gather no dust."
– Jesse Owens

"You find out who your real friends are when you're involved in a scandal."
– Elizabeth Taylor

"Friendship is the only cement that will ever hold the world together."
– Woodrow T. Wilson

"Friends are those rare people who ask how we are and then wait to hear the answer."
– Ed Cunningham

"Anybody can sympathise with the sufferings of a friend, but it requires a very fine nature to sympathise with a friend's success."
– Oscar Wilde

"We cannot tell the precise moment when friendship is formed. As in filling a vessel drop by drop, there is at last a drop which makes it run over; so in a series of kindnesses there is at last one which makes the heart run over."
– Ray Bradbury

"Friendship is inexplicable, it should not be explained if one doesn't want to kill it."
– Max Jacob

"True friendship can afford true knowledge. It does not depend on darkness and ignorance."
– Henry David Thoreau

"If you can survive 11 days in cramped quarters with a friend and come out laughing, your friendship is the real deal."
– Oprah Winfrey

"Friendship is a word, the very sight of which in print makes heart warm."
– Augustine Birrell

"My best friend is the one who brings out the best in me."
– Henry Ford

"A good friend is like a four-leaf clover: hard to find and lucky to have."
– Irish Proverb

"Of all possessions a friend is the most precious."
– Herodotus

"A friend is what the heart needs all the time."
– Henry Van Dyke

Thanks for reading!

Look out for more Quote-Banana books.